LONDON TRANSPORT RAILWAYS ALBUM

Overleaf: Variety at Wembley Park. New Metropolitan Line A 60 'silver' stock heading for Baker Street contrasts with Bakerloo Line '1938' tube stock and Metropolitan 'P' stock on an Uxbridge working in the early 1960s. The chimneys of Neasden generating station visible in the background have since been demolished.

LONDON TRANSPORT RAILWAYS ALBUM

C. S. Heaps, LL.B

LONDON

IAN ALLAN LTD

First published 1978

ISBN 0 7110 0859 0

© Ian Allan Ltd 1978

Published by Ian Allan Ltd, Shepperton, Surrey;
and printed in the United Kingdom by
Ian Allan Printing Ltd

Introduction

Gallia est omnis divisa in partes tres (Julius Caesar — De Bello Gallico). Like Caesar's Gaul, the development of the London Underground system can be described in three parts, and at the present time it is uncertain whether it is still in the midst of the third stage of its development or whether economic and political pressures may soon herald the end of the latest stage.

Although main-line railways came to London as long ago as 1836, when the first section of the London and Greenwich Railway opened from Deptford to Bermondsey, and main-line termini multiplied soon after, it was not until 1863 that the first urban underground railway in the world opened in the capital. Ever since the coming of the railways to London, however, plans for underground railways in the City had been mooted by Charles Pearson, who was City Solicitor between 1839 and his death in 1862. In the 1830s, a scheme for a railway from Kings Cross to Snow Hill (near St Bartholomew's Hospital and the Old Bailey) had been put forward; in 1845 a project for a line in tunnel between the Great Western Railway at Paddington and the Eastern Counties Railway at Shoreditch under the New Road (later known as Marylebone Road and Euston Road) had been proposed; and in 1851 a Committee had been set up to consider Pearson's 'Railway Terminus and City Improvement Plan' in which he conceived a 100ft wide road from Holborn to Kings Cross which would be supported on the arches of a tunnel wide enough to take no less than six standard gauge and two broad gauge railway tracks! Despite approval by the Court of Common Council, the plan foundered through lack of support from the main-line companies, but by 1853 parliamentary sanction had been obtained for the 'North Metropolitan Railway' to be built between Paddington and Kings Cross. The project was reincorporated as the 'Metropolitan Railway' in 1854.

The line opened on 10 January 1863, sadly just over three months after Pearson's death, and proved an instant success. The Metropolitan Railway rapidly expanded, eastwards to Moorgate Street (later Moorgate) in 1865 and westwards to

Left: In the era of the mini-skirt, as revealed by the station advertisements, new Victoria Line stock enters Seven Sisters station in 1968.

South Kensington in 1868. Here the Metropolitan Railway met end-on with the 'Metropolitan District Railway' (incorporated in 1864) which opened between South Kensington and Westminster Bridge on Christmas Eve 1868, and itself later extended eastwards under the newly constructed Embankment to Blackfriars in 1870 and westwards 'into the country' (as it then was) to Hammersmith in 1874. Later still, exercising running rights over the tracks of the London and South Western Railway, the Metropolitan District Railway, or District as it was commonly called, extended to Richmond and Wimbledon. The Metropolitan Railway also steadily extended its scope of operation, to the west over the Hammersmith and City Rly in 1865 and to the north to Swiss Cottage in 1868 via the Metropolitan and St John's Wood Railway. In the latter part of the nineteenth century the Metropolitan, with main-line aspirations inspired after 1872 by its Chairman Sir Edward Watkin (1819-1901), forged northward into Buckinghamshire, eventually to terminate over 50 miles from Baker Street at the rural outposts of Brill and Verney Junction.

The Metropolitan and Metropolitan District Railways were keen rivals during the early years, but they were eventually required by Parliament in 1884 to complete the 'Inner Circle' by constructing the missing link between Aldgate and Mansion House, and thereafter the two companies began to work in the greater harmony necessitated by the joint working of the Inner Circle system (known as the 'Circle' in early days).

The growth of the Metropolitan and Metropolitan District Railways constitutes the first part of the development of the underground system. The second chapter in the saga dates from 1890, after which date the 'tube railways' which eventually made up the Northern, Bakerloo, Central and Piccadilly lines were developed. The Metropolitan and District systems had been built by the 'cut and cover' method, but the new lines were built deep in the London clay. This development was made possible by the invention of the Greathead Shield, which excavated a circular tunnel through the clay to be lined with cast-iron segments. The first tube line was opened in 1890 between King William Street and Stockwell by the City and South London Railway, and was soon followed in 1900 by the first section of the Central London Railway between Shepherds Bush and Bank; in 1906 by the Baker Street and Waterloo Railway between Baker Street and North Lambeth; also in 1906 by the Great Northern, Piccadilly and Brompton Railway between Hammersmith and Finsbury Park; and in 1907 by the Charing Cross,

Euston and Hampstead Railway between Strand and Golders Green and Archway.

Although originally planned by separate companies, by 1902 the Bakerloo, Piccadilly and Hampstead lines had all come within the control of one man, Charles Tyson Yerkes, who had acquired the District Railway in 1901. They were all amalgamated as the London Electric Railway in 1910. London is indebted to C. T. Yerkes, an American (1837-1905) from Chicago, for the greater part of its inner underground system, and it is ironic that the only other person who has had as much influence on the development of the London Underground was also brought up in the United States of America. Albert Henry Knattriess, whose family surname was later changed to Stanley, was born in Derby in 1874 but shortly afterwards moved with his family to America. After speedy promotion in the service of The Public Service Corporation of New Jersey, Albert Stanley was invited back to the United Kingdom in 1910 as Managing Director of the London Electric Railway and, as Baron Ashfield of Southwell (created 1920), became the first Chairman of the London Passenger Transport Board in 1933 and retained the Chairmanship almost until Nationalisation in 1947.

Mention of Lord Ashfield develops the story of the London Underground to the formation of the LPTB in 1933; on 1 July 1933 the LPTB acquired the undertakings of the Underground Group (which included the former City & South London Railway, the Central London Railway, the London Electric Railway and the Metropolitan District Railway) and the Metropolitan Railway (ie all the underground lines except the Southern Railway's Waterloo and City line). Since that date, between 1948 and 1963 under the name of the London Transport Executive, between 1963 and 1969 as The London Transport Board and since 1970 vested in the London Executive, the underground railway system has remained in common ownership and (especially in recent years) has presented an increasingly unified appearance.

The tube railway boom which commenced in 1890 was most active before the commencement of World War I. In the 1920s and 1930s the tube lines were extended to the north and west, often above ground using existing lines of the main-line companies and even after World War II the Central Line was extended over partly new and partly ex-LNER tracks eastwards as far as Ongar. Certain developments proposed in the 1935-1940 New Works Scheme were halted by World War II and later extinguished by planning legislation and the creation of 'green belts'.

Below: With its crew enjoying little protection from the elements, Metropolitan Railway Class A 4-4-0T No 59 heads a Rickmansworth train through the future suburbs of North London.

Below right: C 69 stock on Hammersmith and City Line duties approaches Paddington in September 1975.

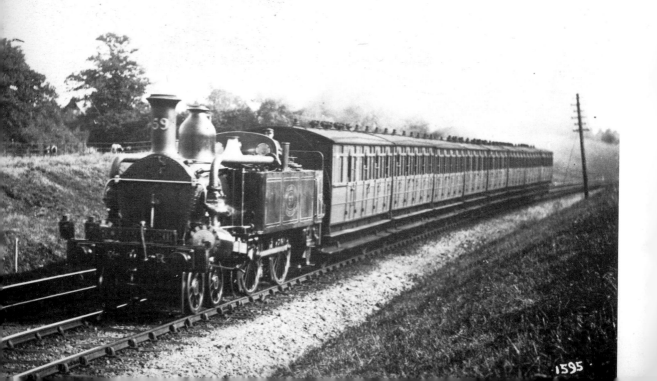

The third era of underground construction commenced in the early 1960s with the authorisation of the construction of the Victoria Line in 1962. Originally proposed (with detailed variations) as Route C in the Report of the Working Party set up to consider the effects of the scheme proposed by the Railway (London Plan) Committee for postwar London, construction work commenced in September 1962 and the first section opened between Walthamstow Central and Highbury and Islington on 1 September 1968. Operations were extended to Warren Street three months later and the important section thence to Victoria was opened by Her Majesty the Queen on 7 March 1969. A further section to Brixton, authorised in 1967, was opened in 1971.

The Piccadilly Line extension to Heathrow Airport, which opened on 16 December 1977, was authorised in 1970, and the Jubilee Line (originally known as the Fleet Line), now under construction between Baker Street and Strand (now known as Charing Cross), was sanctioned in the following year. It remains to be seen whether these sections will mark the conclusion of the third era of construction or whether, as is to be hoped, a rolling plan of underground construction will continue to attract Government and GLC financial support.

Whether or not further development takes place, however, there can be no denying the importance of the underground system to London, its inhabitants and commuters. New stock is being, or has been, introduced on all lines to improve the lot of the underground traveller, and modern techniques such as automatic trains on the Victoria and Jubilee Lines help both to increase the impressive safety record of the system and to reduce staff and operating costs.

In this book, I have endeavoured to illustrate the development of the underground system with contemporary photographs. I have not set out to produce a book of 'pretty pictures' but have chosen photographs which I hope show, as clearly as possible, the developments that are briefly described in the text. In the preparation of the book, I have been assisted by the officers of the London Underground Railway Society and I am greatly indebted to London Transport for the assistance that I have been afforded by their staff in general, and by their Press Officer (Kenneth Pope), their publicity department and the Manager of the London Transport Collection at Syon Park (John Day) in particular.

John Day is well known as the author of the London Transport publication *The Story of London's Underground* and I hope that this illustrated book may be of interest to readers of, and may be referred to in conjunction with, that definitive work and the numerous high quality books and brief histories produced by London Transport, without which my task would have been impossible.

Dorking, Surrey

C. S. Heaps
December 1977

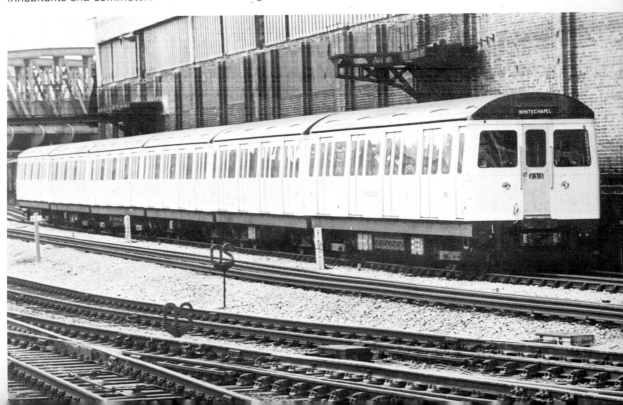

The Early Years

The opening of the first 3¾-mile section of the Metropolitan Railway between Paddington (Bishop's Road) and Farringdon Street on Saturday 10 January 1863 gave London the first underground railway system in the world.

After the abortive projects of the 1830s and 1840s, it was a scheme that first saw the light of day in 1853 that eventually developed into the Metropolitan Railway experiment. The Bayswater, Paddington and Holborn Bridge Railway held its first directors' meeting exactly 10 years before the 1863 opening and appointed John (afterwards Sir John) Fowler (1817-1898) as its Engineer-in-Chief. The Act of Incorporation, which received the Royal Assent on 15 August 1853, authorised the construction of the North Metropolitan Railway (as it had then become) between Kings Cross and Paddington, and the following year further statutory powers were obtained for a line as far as Farringdon Street, in accordance with plans originally proposed by Charles Pearson's City Terminus Company. Although authorised by Parliament, lack of financial support (aggravated no doubt by the Crimean War) resulted in no work being commenced until Pearson persuaded the City Corporation and the Great Western Railway to subscribe for the first 20 per cent of the required capital.

By the end of 1859 the necessary capital had been raised and the first construction contracts were awarded in December. Work commenced almost immediately. The scale and impact of the works can be clearly seen in (1), and in the contemporary print (2) illustrating the constructions of Aldersgate Street Station on the extension to Moorgate (then known as Moorgate Street) opened in late 1865.

The railway was built by the 'cut-and-cover' method in which the cuttings were dug out and later covered over where necessary, and the railway followed so far as possible the lines of existing streets (eg Marylebone Road) to reduce costs and to avoid legal complications. The cuttings and tunnels were constructed to accept two mixed gauge lines, agreements for running powers having been reached with the Great Northern Railway, built on the standard gauge of 4ft 8½in, and the Great Western Railway, which favoured Brunel's broad gauge of 7ft 0¼in.

The biggest engineering feature of the initial length of line was the Clerkenwell Tunnel, which was built between November 1860 and May 1862, in which the line is at its deepest point almost 60ft below the surface. In the construction of the line, work was disrupted by the breaching of the Fleet sewer which broke through the retaining wall and flooded the workings in June 1862 (3) but, surprisingly perhaps, this was the only serious accident that occurred.

The construction works attracted great attention from the

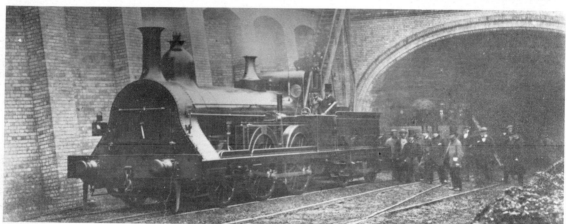

public, as evidenced by the well known inspection carried out by influential local land-owners and politicians on 24 May 1862 illustrated in (**4**). The locomotive which appears on the far left of (**4**) is believed to be Fowler's 'Ghost', an experimental fireless locomotive designed by Fowler and constructed by Robert Stephenson & Co of Newcastle in 1861. The 2-4-0 locomotive (**5**) was designed to run in the ordinary way on open sections of the line and to rely upon dampened down hot fire-bricks in the covered section. The locomotive ran trials on the Great Western Railway in October 1861 and also in the tunnels between Kings Cross and Edgware Road, at which point photograph (**5**) was taken, but the trials proved unsatisfactory and the locomotive was ultimately sold.

Notwithstanding the failure of the 'Ghost', locomotives were required for the opening in 1863 and the directors of the Metropolitan Railway requested help from Daniel (later Sir Daniel) Gooch, Locomotive Superintendent of the GWR, who designed the 2-4-0T locomotives with which the service commenced. These locomotives were built to the broad gauge, and an example is seen in the contemporary print (**6**) of Kings Cross Metropolitan Station shortly after the opening. On the left can be seen an example of the Great Western eight-wheeled

carriage of the type known as 'Long Charleys' which were also designed by Gooch and provided a high standard of comfort for their day.

Relations with the GWR speedily deteriorated, however, problems being exacerbated both by the Great Western's desire for through trains to its system as opposed to the Metropolitan's increasing short distance traffic, and by personality clashes. After issuing an ultimatum that the GWR would no longer work the traffic after 30 September 1863, broad gauge stock was withdrawn on 11 August, and the Metropolitan found it necessary to hire standard gauge locomotives and stock until new replacement locomotives and coaches could be provided. From 1 October, the Great Northern Railway started running through trains to Farringdon Street and, to deal with increased Great Northern traffic, it soon became necessary for the line to be quadrupled between Kings Cross and Moorgate. New 'Widened Lines' were built between November 1865 and May 1867 which passed beneath the original formation at the eastern end of Clerkenwell Tunnel under an unusual wrought iron bridge known as the 'Ray Street Gridiron' which can clearly be seen in contemporary print (**7**).

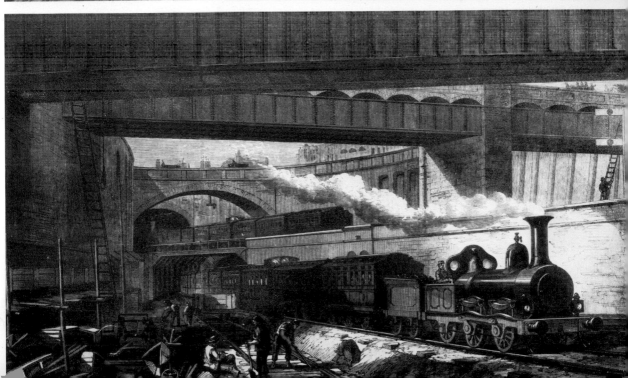

8

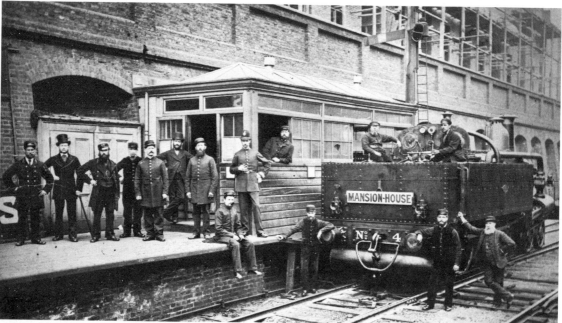

9

10

Metropolitan Steam

To replace the broad-gauge GWR locomotives, Fowler ordered new locomotives for the Metropolitan Railway from Beyer Peacock & Co Limited of Manchester, who adapted a design for locomotives recently supplied to a railway in Spain to meet the Metropolitan's need. The first of 18 handsome 4-4-0T locomotives was delivered in June 1864. When delivered, the first 18 locomotives were finished in a bright green livery, with copper tops and brass figures on the chimney, and bore classical names. The name-plates were eventually removed, and few photographs remain illustrating the locomotives in their original state as shown in (**8**). The locomotives were known as the A type, but the following B type was very similar and the two classes totalled 66 engines, one of which (No 23) is now preserved in the London Transport collection at Syon Park. When the District Railway required motive power, it took delivery of a further 54 similar locomotives from the same builders.

In (**9**) Metropolitan District Locomotive No 4 is shown at the original Earls Court Station in May 1876 and, with later modifications, in (**10**) hauling a District Railway train to Wimbledon at East Ham in (probably) 1905. The A and B class locomotives were used not only on the Inner Circle services but also, after 1884, on the East London Railway to New Cross and New Cross Gate (**11**) and on the Northern extensions of the Metropolitan to Harrow and beyond. In (**12**) Metropolitan Railway No 3 (originally named *Juno*) is seen in rural surroundings near Wembley Park on a Harrow train in 1896.

11

2

More Metropolitan Steam

To cope with the increasingly main-line characteristics of the Metropolitan Line leading north from Baker Street towards Harrow (reached in 1880) and beyond, new tank locomotives were built in small classes for this express work. The line was extended to Aylesbury in 1892, and there joined up with the Aylesbury and Buckingham Railway which had been absorbed in the previous year. Save for five powerful 0-6-0 locomotives built in 1868 for the extension to Swiss Cottage, which were soon found to be too powerful and were sold, the first locomotives to depart from the original A class design were not built until 1891 when the C class was introduced. This class was made up of four 0-4-4T locomotives designed by James Stirling and similar to his design for the South Eastern Railway, one of which (No 69) is shown in (**13**) preparing to head a train to the Metropolitan's furthest outpost at Verney Junction. Their introduction on 4 June 1891 was marred by an accident on that date when No 67 was involved in an accident in the tunnels near Marlborough Road.

The next class to be introduced appeared in 1894/5, when six D class 2-4-0T locomotives were built, two for work on the Aylesbury/Verney Junction section and four (fitted with condensing gear) for use mainly between Baker Street and Aylesbury. The locomotives, which closely resembled a design for the Barry Railway, were built by Sharpe, Stewart, but proved insufficiently powerful for main line passenger work and were used mainly on branch line and goods duties (**14**).

More successful was the 0-4-4T E class designed by T. F. Clark, who had been appointed Locomotive Superintendent of the Metropolitan in 1896. The first three locomotives in the class, Nos 77, 78 and 1, were built at Neasden and four more were constructed by Hawthorn, Leslie. No 1, in the livery of and renumbered L44 by London Transport is seen in (**15**) in 1961 hauling an Enthusiasts Special.

In 1897 and 1899, two 0-6-0 saddle tanks were built by Peckett & Sons for yard work at Finchley Road and Harrow (**16**), to be followed in 1901 by four 0-6-2 tanks of the F class built by the Yorkshire Engine Company mainly for freight working. No 91 (later renumbered L50) is seen on goods work in (**17**).

15

16

7

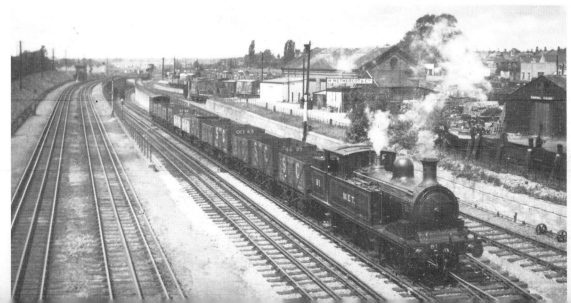

Electrification Experiments

Whilst the Metropolitan Railway had been building new steam locomotive classes for use on its outer-suburban or main lines, the City and South London Railway had opened between King William Street and Stockwell using electric traction. The success of this experiment encouraged both the Metropolitan and the District Railways to consider the electrification of their lines, particularly the Inner Circle, and in 1898 the two companies jointly financed an experiment on the District Railway from High Street, Kensington to Earls Court. A temporary generating station was built at Warwick Road, Earls Court, to provide 600 volts dc, and a new 6-car train was constructed for the tests by Brown, Marshalls & Company in 1899. The experimental train (**18**) ran for the first time on Saturday 9 December 1899 and began an experimental service in May 1900. In November of that year, having been considered a sufficient success to persuade both companies to contemplate general electrification, it was withdrawn from service.

The Metropolitan Railway favoured a 3,000-volt 3-phase alternating current system using overhead wires, a system not yet in operation anywhere in the world, and initially the scheme was accepted by the Joint Electrification Committee of both railways. Later, however, the District withdrew its support for this scheme after it had come under the control of Charles Yerkes, whose engineers were not in favour of adopting an untried system. After an Arbitration Tribunal, the dispute was settled in favour of the low-voltage dc system favoured by Yerkes.

The District Railway, unencumbered with outer suburban and express services, showed greater enthusiasm for electrification than the Metropolitan and undertook initial electrification work between Acton and South Harrow at the very beginning of the twentieth century. The first section was brought into operation between Mill Hill Park and Park Royal on 23 June 1903 to provide a service to the nearby Royal Agricultural Show. Five days later a through service to South Harrow began using A class seven-car trains built by the Brush Electrical Engineering Company of Loughborough (**19**). Strong American influence can be seen in the design of the original class of electric stock, which remained in service until 1925. The experiment proved successful and, in 1903, the District Railway placed orders for 420 new cars, classified B stock, to electrify the whole system; the majority of these cars were built in France (**20**).

19

20

23

24

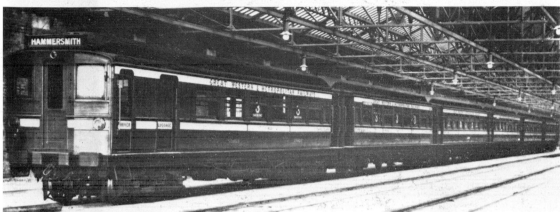

The Metropolitan did not remain idle, however, and introduced electric multiple unit operation at the beginning of 1905 between Baker Street and Uxbridge. In (**21**) one of the first electric units is seen on trial in December 1904. The rear view clearly shows the gate ends with which the stock was originally fitted but which were soon modified. (**22**) shows an early multiple unit train in service.

The Metropolitan also increased its electric coaching stock by converting 'bogie' or 'Ashbury' locomotive-hauled coaches (built between 1898 and 1900) to electric working. Between 1906 and 1924 all the bogie stock was converted, and a seven-car train is shown in (**23**) outside Neasden Shed in Metropolitan Livery.

On the Hammersmith and City Line, services were changed over to electric traction during November and December 1906, when new six-car trains operated in the joint names of the Great Western and Metropolitan Railways were introduced (**24**). The stock was painted in Metropolitan style, and remained in service until 1936.

Main-Line Electrification

Whereas the Distict Railway provided a relatively short distance inner urban service on the Inner Circle and its branches and could contemplate the complete electrification of its system, the Metropolitan Railway by the turn of the century had extended over 50 miles from Baker Street and provided, in part, a less frequent main-line or outer suburban service which could not justify electrification. The Metropolitan wished, however, to eliminate all steam working into Baker Street and 10 Bo-Bo electric locomotives were ordered from British Westinghouse Electric & Manufacturing Company and delivered ready for service by April 1906. The locomotives were 'camel-backed' and, in their early years, sported a very distinctive feature, a large roller destination blind displaying 12in lettering at each end of the locomotive, a feature that is clearly visible on locomotive No 1 illustrated in (**25**). The locomotive is hauling 'bogie' or 'Ashbury' coaches, some of which were already being converted at that time to electric working. The destination blinds proved troublesome and were quickly removed.

Experimental haulage of steam trains by electric locomotives began in 1906 and, from 1 November, all trains were electrically hauled from Baker Street as far as Wembley Park where steam locomotives were attached. The Locomotive exchange point was transferred to Harrow-on-the-Hill in 1908, and to Rickmansworth in January 1925, upon completion of electrification to those points.

A further 10 locomotives were ordered in 1906 from the same builders, although differing externally and materially from the original class. The box-like appearance of the second generation of electric locomotives is clearly shown in (**26**) which shows the prototype No 11 at Willesden Green Junction signal box.

Far more well known is the third class of electric locomotives introduced by the Metropolitan Railway after World War I. Although described at the time as rebuilds of the original locomotives, it is now generally accepted that they were new locomotives ordered after a trial rebuild of No 17 had proved unsatisfactory. No 15 was shown on the Metropolitan Railway Stand at the British Empire Exhibition at Wembley in 1925 and named *Wembley 1924*. The other 19 locomotives were all given names of famous, actual or fictitious, persons connected with the area served by the Metropolitan Railway and then being promoted and publicised as Metroland. In (**27**) No 10 *William*

25

26

27

Ewart Gladstone (later *W. E. Gladstone)* is seen approaching Northwood on a service train in September 1947 whilst (**28**) shows No 18 *Michael Faraday* in London Transport Livery in the late 1950s.

The 'bogie' or 'Ashbury' coaches illustrated in (**25**) behind the prototype Metropolitan Electric Locomotive were replaced in the first decade of the twentieth century on the main-line trains by 'Dreadnought' coaches, of which 92 were built. Two thirds of these remained in use to the end of steam passenger services on London Transport. The 54-foot long Dreadnoughts were compartment coaches incorporating features more usually

associated with main-line rather than underground railway stock, particularly when used in conjunction with the two Pullman cars introduced on the Metropolitan on 1 June 1910 to run between the City or Baker Street and Aylesbury or Chesham (**29**). Two cars, named *Mayflower* and *Galatea* were provided by the Pullman Car Company and furnished to that company's usual high standard. The coaches were initially finished in standard Pullman car livery of umber and cream (**30**), but after their overhaul in 1922/23 the livery was changed to crimson lake as it had been found difficult to maintain the light cream colouring under the Metropolitan's tunnel conditions. The

30

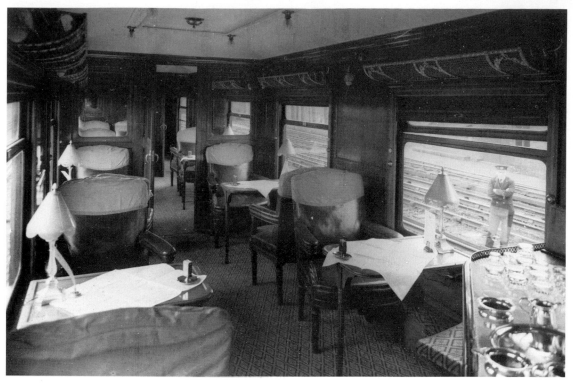

palatial interior illustrated in (**31**) contrasts dramatically with the public image today of underground travel. The Pullman cars were introduced to fight competition from the Great Central Railway trains which began to compete for traffic beyond Harrow-on-the-Hill after the opening of the 'London Extension' in March 1899, a rivalry perhaps best personified by a well-known photograph (**32**) showing an electrically hauled Metropolitan Pullman train running parallel with a Marylebone to Manchester express near Northwick Park hauled by LNER Class B17 4-6-0 No 2816 *Fallodon*. A Pullman car service continued to be provided on the Metropolitan Line even after the formation of the London Passenger Transport Board in 1933 and *Mayflower* and *Galatea* were not withdrawn until 7 October 1939 after the outbreak of World War II. The names chosen for the two Pullman cars were those of two contestant yachts in the 1886 America's Cup.

The use of electric locomotives on the District Line is less well known. Full electric operation of the Inner Circle service jointly by the Metropolitan and District Railways commenced on

24 September 1905, and, to avoid the retention of steam locomotives on through services from the London and North Western Railway between Earls Court and Mansion House, 10 electric locomotives were built by The Metropolitan Amalgamated Railway Carriage & Wagon Company for this purpose. The LNWR operated an 'Outer Circle' service from Broad Street via Willesden Junction and Addison Road (now Olympia) to Earls Court and thence over the District Line to Mansion House. After 1 January 1909, when the Outer Circle service was cut back to Earls Court, the District locomotives were rendered redundant and three were scrapped two years later. The remaining locomotives were used to haul through trains from Ealing to Southend operated by the District Railway in conjunction with the London Tilbury and Southend Railway, on which service the locomotives were coupled in pairs on the electric section between Barking and Ealing Broadway. Two such locomotives are seen leaving Ealing Broadway in (**33**) on the Southend service, which survived until 30 September 1939.

Metropolitan Main-Line Steam

As has already been mentioned, the main-line Metropolitan services were electrically hauled from Baker Street only as far as Harrow-on-the-Hill until 1908 and as far as Rickmansworth from 5 January 1925. Thence to Aylesbury and, until passenger services were withdrawn in 1936, to Verney Junction, the Metropolitan trains were steam hauled to their destination. Increasing traffic necessitated the building of locomotives more powerful than the E and F classes, and in 1915 four G class 0-6-4Ts were introduced numbered 94/5/6/7. (**34**) All four locomotives were graced with names, *Lord Aberconway*, (the Chairman of the Metropolitan Railway), *Robert H. Selbie*, (the General Manager), *Charles Jones* and *Brill*.

The G class was followed five years later by the H class 4-4-4T also designed by Charles Jones and built by Kerr Stuart & Co, the handsome lines of which can clearly be seen in (**35**) and (**36**).

The final type to be introduced was the powerful K class 2-6-4T constructed in 1925 (**37**). The locomotives were designed by George Hally, CME of the Metropolitan since 1923, and incorporated unassembled parts of unbuilt South Eastern and Chatham Railway Class N 2-6-0 locomotives designed and made during World War I at Woolwich Arsenal. The family relationship with the SECR Class N is clearly recognisable, whilst the borrowing of an SECR design is reminiscent of the introduction of the Class C tank locomotives in 1891.

All the Class G, H and K locomotives became part of the London Passenger Transport Board's stock in 1933, but from 1937 responsibility for main-line steam working was transferred to the London and North Eastern Railway and the locomotives in those three classes were absorbed into LNER stock and renumbered.

35

36

37

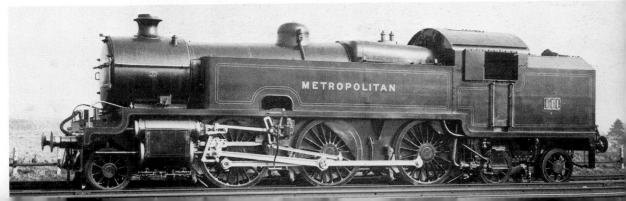

The Brill Branch

The G class locomotive No 97 was named *Brill,* after the
terminus of the strangest line ever to form part of the London
Transport system. Known originally as The Wotton Tramway,
and later as The Oxford and Aylesbury Tramroad, the branch-
line from Quainton Road to Brill in the depths of
Buckinghamshire was constructed for private traffic by the Duke
of Buckingham and opened as far as Wotton on 1 April 1871. It
opened for public service in January of the following year and
two tiny locomotives were built by Aveling and Porter for the
service which were really no more than geared traction engines
complete with fly-wheels but fitted with flanged wheels (**38**).
The locomotives were sold in 1894 when a second-hand 0-6-0
Manning Wardle and Co saddletank named *Huddersfield* (later
renamed *Wotton Number 1*) joined the locomotive stock. This
was joined in the following year by a new 0-6-0T from the same

builders, named *Brill No 2,* which was itself joined four years
later by a sister engine named *Wotton No 2* on the withdrawal
of the second-hand locomotive. In (**39**), *Wotton No 2* is shown
attached to an 1866-built 'Oldbury' coach, part of the original
Metropolitan Railway stock. Despite appearances, the coach is
not a bogie coach !

The Oxford and Aylesbury Tramroad came under the control
of the Metropolitan Railway in December 1899 and, from
2 April 1906, fell within the sphere of influence of the
Metropolitan and Great Central Joint Committee. Two Class A
4-4-0Ts were transferred to the branch by the Metropolitan
Railway (Nos 23 and 41), the former of which is seen at
Quainton Road in (**40**). The line survived to be taken into the
ownership of the London Passenger Transport Board in 1933
and the branch coaches and locomotives were even repainted in
new livery (**41**) but, not surprisingly, the line closed
completely soon afterwards on 30 November 1935.

More Metropolitan Electrification

The extension of electric working to Rickmansworth in 1925 and the opening of the joint Metropolitan and LNER branch to Watford on 2 November 1925 necessitated the construction of additional electric rolling stock for the Metropolitan. A number of new saloon coaches fitted with hand operated doors had been constructed in the 1900s, and in 1913 and 1921 more were built by the Metropolitan Carriage Wagon & Finance

Company for use on the Inner Circle and East London services. A selection of styles is very evident in the trains standing at the Wembley Park Exhibition platforms in (42). In 1933, 90 vehicles were renovated for continued use on the Circle Line. Save for the adoption of a new livery of red and cream (43), the external appearance of the units was little changed and the stock remained in use on the Circle Line until 31 December 1950. (44) shows the last Circle Line car at Aldgate Station on its last day of operation.

For use on the main-line and Watford branch, new

compartment multiple unit stock of the MW and MV (later T) type was ordered in 1927 and 1929, an example of which is illustrated in (**45**) when new on 21 June 1927 at the Watford terminus. Coach No 207 is one of a series provided with side buffers, screw couplings and vacuum brakes for use with steam stock built in 1920/23 to make up seven-coach trains. The vacuum fitted coaches were known as MV stock, but they were converted to the Westinghouse braking system used on the MW stock in 1935.

A unique train, formed in part of MW stock, is illustrated in (**46**) on the occasion of the opening of the Stanmore branch by the Metropolitan Railway on 9 December 1932. In addition to standard MW motor coaches, the train includes one of the two Metropolitan Railway Pullman Cars and the unique Rothschild

Saloon constructed at Neasden Works in 1905 from two special saloon vehicles originally constructed in 1895 for the use of Ferdinand de Rothschild, whose country seat was near Wendover Station. After reconstruction, the saloon was used by the Chairman and Directors of the Metropolitan Railway for line inspections and as a substitute for the company's Pullman cars when necessary.

The MW or T stock remained in passenger carrying service until October 1962, and units even saw service on the newly electrified sections to Amersham and Chesham, pending receipt of the final deliveries of the new stock ordered for such extension. (**47**) illustrates a unit in London Transport service in the early 1950s.

46

47

The East London Railway

As already mentioned, Metropolitan and District Railway Services had commenced on the East London line to New Cross in 1884, but the line had opened as early as 6 December 1869 between the London, Brighton & South Coast Railway Station at New Cross (now New Cross Gate) and Wapping. The line was built in the tunnel under the River Thames originally designed by the father of Isambard Kingdom Brunel, Sir Marc Isambard Brunel, and opened for pedestrian use in March 1843, almost 20 frustrating years after work first began. The tunnel was not a financial success and it was purchased by the East London Railway (Incorporated in May 1865) for £200,000 in 1865. The tunnel is seen in (**48**) in its original state, and the entrance can be seen to be but little changed when put to the railway use illustrated in (**49**). Today the scene is much as shown in (**50**), although the ex-District Railway F stock there illustrated was subsequently replaced by 1938 standard tube stock and, in 1977, by A60 Metropolitan Line trains.

The East London Railway was physically connected to the LBSCR at New Cross Gate, to the SER at New Cross and to the GER at Bishopsgate. Through services between Liverpool Street and New Croydon (the then name of part of the station now known as East Croydon) used the line between 1876 and 1885, and the LBSCR provided a Shoreditch-Peckham Rye service until 1911, but since 1975 all connections with British Railways have been severed. Despite its London Transport appearance, however, the ELR until Nationalisation of the railways in 1948 was only 35 per cent owned by LPTB (as successors to the District and Metropolitan Railways). 47½ per cent of the shares were held by the Southern Railway and 17½ per cent by the LNER.

Contact with British Railways at New Cross Gate is illustrated (**51**), which shows a Ramblers 'special' headed by ex-Metropolitan Railway electric locomotive No 14 *Benjamin Disraeli* and ex-LBSCR 0-6-0 Class C2X No 32543 in June 1956.

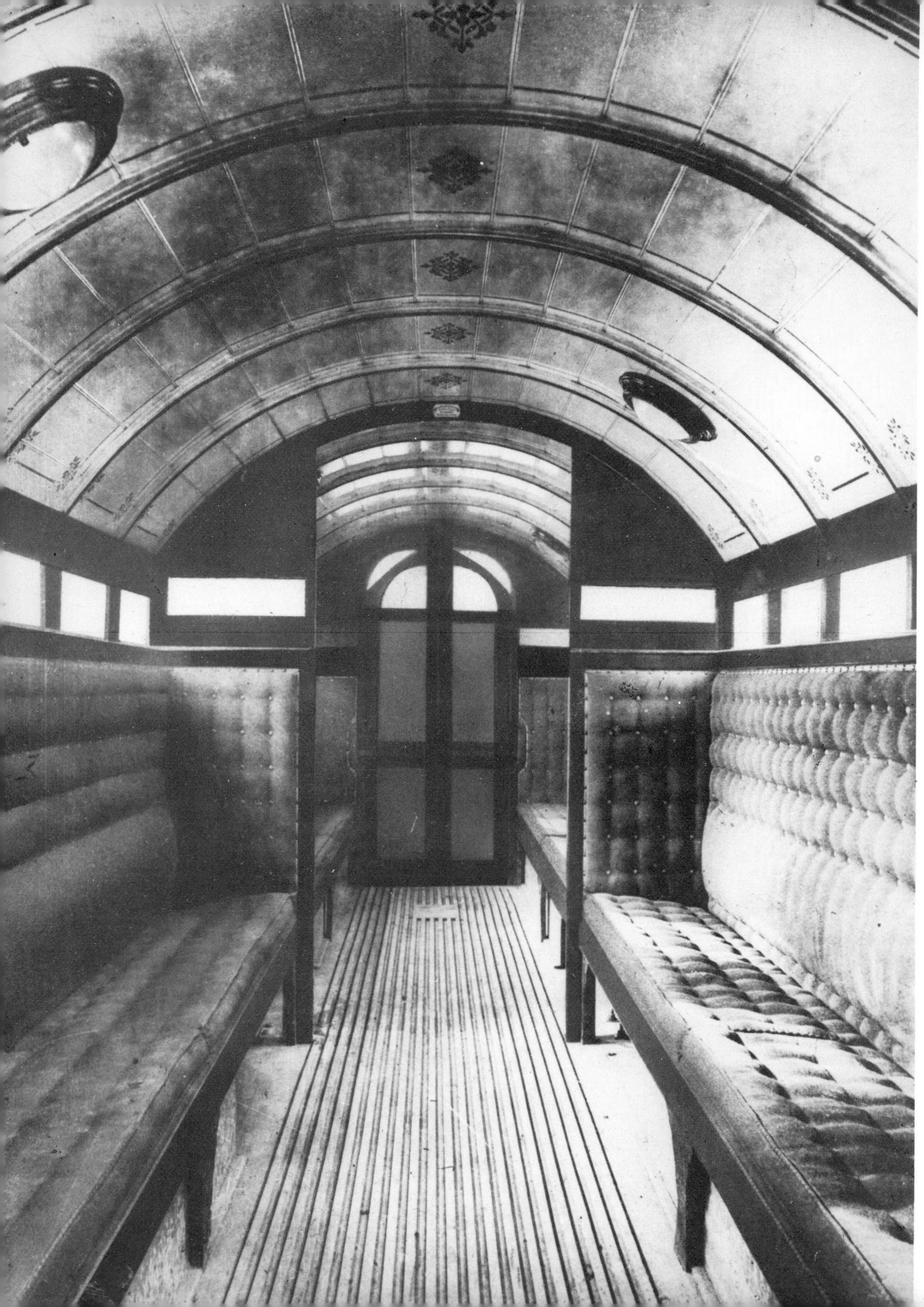

53

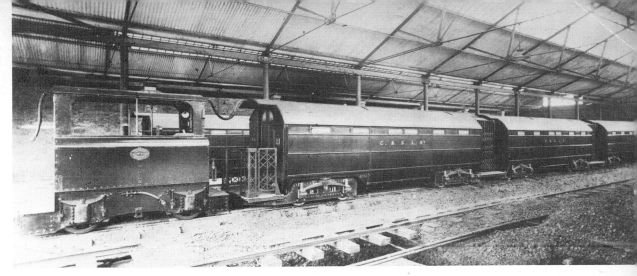

The City and South London Railway

In 1868, the Tower Subway Company had been formed to build a 'tube tunnel' beneath the River Thames using an idea patented by its Engineer, Peter William Barlow, and later developed by his pupil, James Henry Greathead, for cutting through London clay and lining the excavations with iron tubes. The tunnel was built successfully and on 2 August 1870 a passenger service commenced beneath the river on a cable-hauled 2ft 6in gauge railway. This, the first tube railway in the world, was not a financial success and ceased operation after but a few months, the tubes thereafter being used as a pedestrian subway and, after 1894, to carry water mains for the Metropolitan Water Board. Despite its financial failure, the Tower Subway Company had proved the feasibility of building tube tunnels under London and the City of London and Southwark Subway Company was incorporated in 1884 (with Greathead as the Engineer) to build a railway line from King William Street to Elephant. Works

began in February 1886, when cable haulage was still proposed but the directors of the company were inspired by the success of the Volks Electric Railway at Brighton in 1883 and decided to use electric traction. The line (by now extended to Stockwell) was formally opened by the Prince of Wales (later King Edward VII) on 4 November 1890, although the public service did not commence until a little over a month later. The trains were made up of four locomotive-hauled coaches immediately nicknamed 'padded cells' because of the small size of the windows that were initially provided for ventilation only. The claustrophobic interior is very evident in (**52**). The original locomotive and coaching stock is illustrated in (**53**). The first batch of 14 locomotives was built by Mather & Platt, and 38 additional locomotives had also been delivered by 1907, the coaching stock having increased from 30 to 165 vehicles. The original coaches were later rebuilt with windows. In (**54**) original locomotive No 8 (as rebuilt in 1907 at the Stockwell Works of the Railway) is seen hauling more modern coaching stock on the extension to Euston which opened in that year.

54

The Central London Railway

The Prince of Wales (later King Edward VII) obviously showed a keen interest in the development of the London underground system for, 10 years after the opening of the C&SLR, he officiated at the opening of the Central London Railway between Shepherds Bush and Bank (**55**). Initially dubbed 'the twopenny tube', by reason of its standard 2d fare, and referred to as such in the contemporary revival of the Gilbert & Sullivan Opera *Patience,* the Central London Railway had been incorporated in August 1891 and commenced construction works four years later. The public service was introduced using locomotive-hauled coaches, a train of one of which is illustrated in (**56**). The interior is illustrated in (**57**). Unfortunately, within the first six months of service, complaints were received that the 44-ton locomotives were causing vibration disturbances to the buildings on the line of the route and a Committee was set up by the Board of Trade to investigate. Even before the Report of the Committee was published in February 1902, the company had commenced experiments with multiple unit trains, as the result of which it was decided to replace the locomotive hauled service with multiple units, a change-over completed by June 1903. One of the new units is illustrated in (**58**).

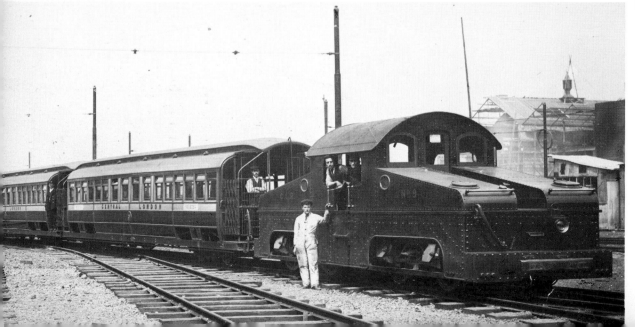

The Great Northern & City Railway

The Central London Railway enjoyed the honour of introducing the first multiple unit service in Europe, but only just. Whilst the CLR was experimenting with multiple unit operations and awaiting the outcome of the Board of Trade enquiry, the Directors of the Great Northern and City Railway (authorised in 1892) had already decided to introduce multiple unit trains on their new 3.42-mile line between Finsbury Park and Moorgate. Construction work commenced in 1898 and the line opened on 14 February 1904. Despite financial problems, the expensive decision was reached by the company to construct its tunnels to a diameter of 16ft, sufficient to accommodate main-line rolling stock, notwithstanding that the Great Northern Railway had reneged on an earlier agreement to permit through running from its main-line.

The generous tunnel loading gauge, however, permitted the construction of stock of handsome proportions as illustrated in (**59**) and (**60**). The third class trailer car No 164 illustrated in (**60**) is decked out in the livery of the Metropolitan Railway, by whom the assets of the company were acquired on 30 June 1913. The main-line sized stock was replaced by tube stock in 1939.

Under the 1935/40 London Transport Improvement Programme, the Alexandra Palace branch of the LNER was to have been electrified and operated as an extension of the GN&C line, but these plans were interrupted by World War II and thereafter abandoned. The original far-sightedness of the Directors in building the line to main-line rather than tube standards has, however, been justified after over 70 years. From 8 November 1976, the line was incorporated in the BR Great Northern Electrification Scheme and is now served solely by British Railways Electric Stock (**61**). As from 6 November 1976, the Great Northern Suburban Services ceased to use the Widened Lines to Moorgate over which they had operated since 1863, although the future of the Widened Lines should be assured by their inclusion in the St Pancras-Bedford electrification scheme announced by British Railways on the very first weekday after the GN services ended.

The terminus of the GN&CR branch at Moorgate, in its final months of operation as part of the London Transport system, was the scene of the worst accident in the history of London's Underground when, on 28 February 1975, a six-car train failed to stop at the terminal station and 42 passengers and the driver lost their lives in the resulting impact into the end of the dead-end tunnel.

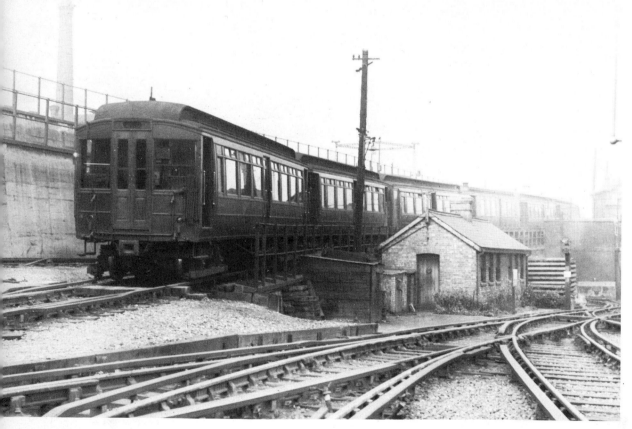

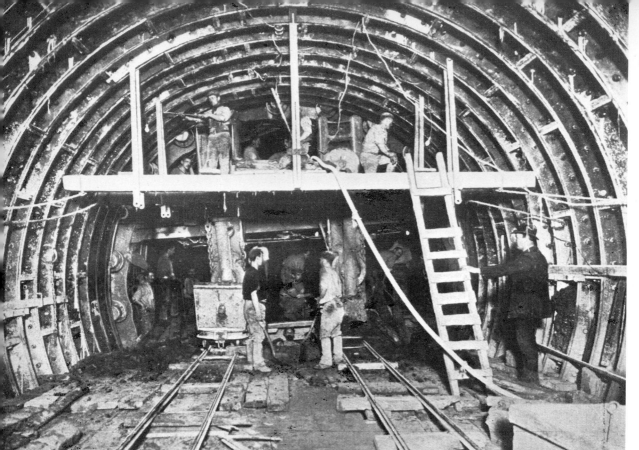

The Bakerloo Line

Two years after the opening of the GN&CR the Baker Street and Waterloo Railway — almost instantly and thereafter known as the Bakerloo — opened on 10 March 1906 between Baker Street and Kennington Road (now known as Lambeth North). The line was extended southwards to Elephant and Castle in August of that year and to the north to Edgware Road in 1907. A branch to Paddington was opened in 1913 and extended thence to Queens Park in 1915 and to Watford Junction two years later.

(**62**) illustrates the construction of the tunnels at Edgware Road using the Greathead shield system and (**63**) illustrates the prototype scarlet and white liveried all-steel motor coach No 1 built by the American Car & Foundry Company in the USA and assembled in Manchester. For the extension to Watford Junction, new six-car trains built to the joint design of the London & North Western Railway and the London Electric Railway (of which the Bakerloo was a part) were provided (**64**) and painted in the chocolate and cream livery of the LNWR. The trains were a compromise design, with the floors of the carriages 4½in higher than in ordinary tube stock as the trains served not only tube railway platforms, but also main-line railway platforms on the LNWR lines beyond Queens Park. When the service was introduced, not all the new stock was available and coaches were borrowed from the Piccadilly Line and from the Central London Railway, one of whose motor coaches can be seen in (**65**) about to be overtaken by an LNWR express and in (**66**).

64

65

66

The Piccadilly & Hampstead Lines

Ten months after the opening of the Bakerloo, another tube railway opened in London when, on 15 December 1906, the Great Northern Piccadilly and Brompton Railway opened between Hammersmith and Finsbury Park. At the time of its opening, it enjoyed the distinction of being the longest tube railway in London, the result of an amalgamation of various separate schemes that had been developed by C. T. Yerkes. In the west, the line between Brompton and Piccadilly Circus had been authorised in 1897, whilst in the north-east the Great Northern and Strand Railway had been incorporated in 1899 with a view to operating a line between Wood Green, Finsbury Park and Strand. No construction work commenced on either line until the powers of the Brompton and Piccadilly Circus Railway and the Great Northern and Strand Railway were purchased by Yerkes and reconstituted, together with the Bakerloo, as the Underground Electric Railways Company of London Ltd. The Great Northern and Strand Railway was vested in the Brompton and Piccadilly Circus Railway by Act of Parliament in August 1902, and a subsequent Act in November of that year sanctioned the change of name to the Great Northern Piccadilly and Brompton Railway and authorised the connecting link between Piccadilly and Holborn.

The main-line from Finsbury Park to Hammersmith was opened by the President of the Board of Trade, The Rt Hon David Lloyd George, on 15 December 1906 and the line was worked by rolling stock generally similar in design to that already in operation on the Bakerloo. Nearly all the stock was built in France or Hungary and an example of the 1905 stock is shown in (**67**). The stock was finished in Midland Lake Livery.

Only six months later, on 22 June 1907, the Charing Cross

Euston & Hampstead Railway was opened between Strand and Golders Green and Highgate (now Archway). The Hampstead tube (as it was generally known) was incorporated by an Act of Parliament of August 1893 and the statutory powers were purchased by C. T. Yerkes for £100,000 in 1900. Construction work on the Hampstead line began in September 1903 and finished in December 1905. Deep tunnelling was required in places as, for instance, where the line passed beneath Hampstead Heath over 190ft below the surface. The construction of the station at Charing Cross was complicated by the refusal of the South Eastern & Chatham to permit any disturbance of the forecourt at its Charing Cross terminus but, in the event, the problem was solved for the Hampstead tube by the collapse of the arched roof of Charing Cross main-line Station and the subsequent closure of the station for over three months, during which period the necessary works were carried out. Until an extension was built in 1926 southwards from Charing Cross to join the City and South London Railway at Kennington, the southern extremity of the Hampstead tube was a loop at Charing Cross which is illustrated on the track diagram in (**68**) which shows the interior of the 1907 original Hampstead rolling stock. The external appearance of the original gate stock is shown in (**69**) which illustrates a train of the original stock forming a business service introduced on 13 November 1911 to run non-stop from Hampstead to Euston.

Both branches of the Hampstead tube were extended in the 1920s, from Golders Green to Hendon in 1923 and thence to Edgware in the following year, and from Archway to East Finchley (using ex-LNER tracks) in July 1939. In (**70**) a train of new London Electric Railway stock is seen on trial over the new extension line to Edgware, whilst (**71**) illustrates a rural Hendon Central at the time of the extension to Edgware in August 1924.

69

70

71

Tube Expansion and Modernisation

As we have already seen, C. T. Yerkes purchased the powers for the Charing Cross, Euston & Hampstead Railway in 1900 and in the following year secured control of the District Railway, to be followed soon after by the purchase of the Brompton and Piccadilly Circus Railway, the Great Northern and Strand and the Bakerloo. In 1902, the Yerkes Group formed the Underground Electric Railways Company of London Limited, and in 1910 all the lines were amalgamated under the name of the London Electric Railway. The extensions of the Bakerloo to Watford and Edgware were matched by extensions on the Piccadilly Line from Finsbury Park to Cockfosters (reached in 1933) and, by the quadrupling of the District Line section between Hammersmith and Northfields, to Hounslow from South Harrow and Uxbridge. (**72**) illustrates a train of standard London Electric Railway stock leaving the south end of Southgate tunnel (opened in 1933) and (**73**) shows the interior of an LER trailer coach introduced for the 1933 extensions. A full train of 1931/34 standard stock is illustrated in (**74**) at Lillie Bridge Depot, on the site now occupied by the Cromwell Road

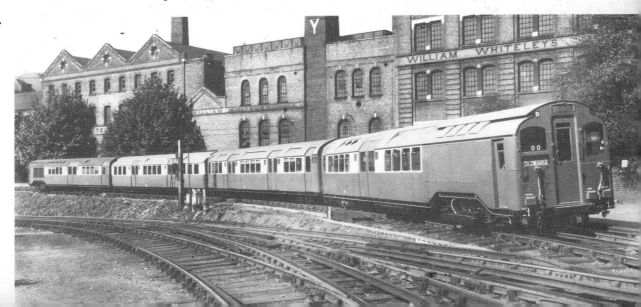

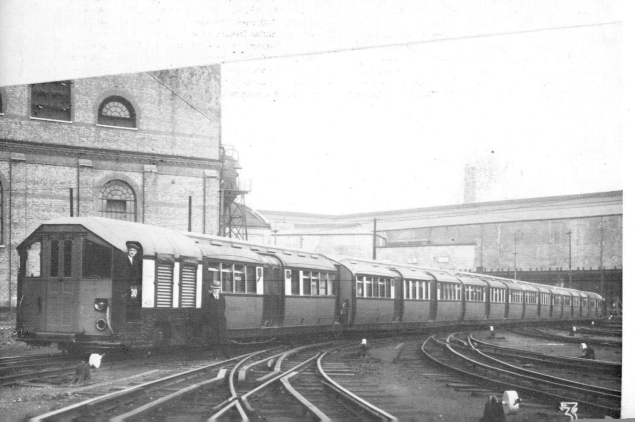

extension, whilst (**76**) shows a Bakerloo Line train headed by a 1927 Feltham stock motor coach distinguished by the characteristic curve of the lower body panels.

Standard stock was to be found on the Bakerloo, Piccadilly and Northern Lines, although only after 1924 on the original section of the City and South London Railway which was reconstructed after temporary closure between 1922 and 1924 to permit the tunnels to be enlarged from their original 10ft 2in diameter to the standard minimum of 11ft 8¼in. On the Central

London line, however, that Company's unique stock — although reconstructed in 1926/28 to air-door working (**76**) — remained in use until 1940, when it was found possible to convert the line to standard London Transport fourth-rail electric practice.

The last standard stock was withdrawn by London Transport in 1966, after which 51 cars were rehabilitated at Acton Works and sold to the Southern Region of British Railways for use, in surroundings more bracing than they were accustomed to, on newly electrified lines on the Isle of Wight (**77**).

District line F Stock

New stock was constructed for the District Line by the Metropolitan Carriage Wagon & Finance Company in 1920 officially designated 'F' stock but nicknamed 'Dreadnoughts' or 'Tanks'. The F cars were incompatible with existing District Line stock. A five-coach unit is illustrated in (**78**) in its original form outside Ealing Common Depot. Each coach bears 'non-stopping' indicators, which were subsequently removed and are not visible on the Aldgate-Uxbridge train photographed at West Hampstead in June 1962 (**79**). (**80**) illustrates the interior of a first class smoking carriage. In later years, the centre grab poles and compartment dividers were removed and first class abolished. The F class was renovated in 1950 and remained in passenger service on the East London Line (**50**) and Uxbridge services until 1963.

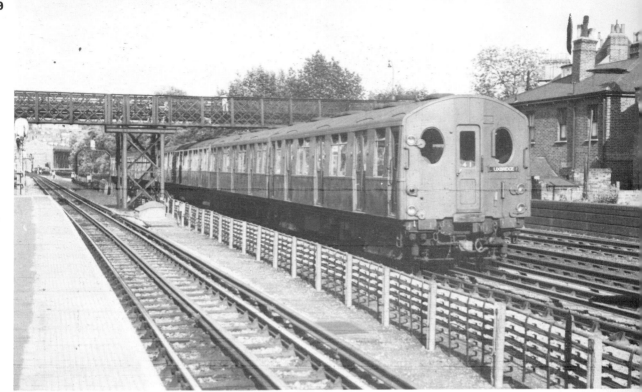

District Line Stock

Further new stock was ordered by the District Railway, this time from the Gloucester Railway Carriage & Wagon Company, in 1923, and 50 motor cars were delivered to enable some of the original wooden trailer cars to be scrapped. The G cars were similar in appearance to earlier District Railway units, with clerestory roofs and straight-sided bodies, and under the 1935/40 New Works programme the G cars were modernised by the fitting of air-operated doors and electro-pneumatic brakes to join the Q stock fleet, a train of which is illustrated in (81) at Farringdon headed by a G (later known as Q27) motor coach. Two 1923 G cars were converted in 1939 for double-ended use on the South Acton-Acton Town 'shuttle' service, on which one

of the units is seen in (82) at the branch terminus shortly before the complete closure of the line in February 1959. Further stock was introduced on the District Line between 1927 and 1935, again built by the Birmingham Railway Carriage & Wagon Company; originally designated 'K' stock, it later was also included in the Q classification. The 1927/35 stock was also constructed with clerestory roofs, but had a less box-like appearance, in the main because the clerestory roofs were rounded off at the front of each coach. Q27 stock is illustrated in (83) at New Cross and (84) at Acton Town.

The 1935 stock was introduced after the formation of the LPTB by whom, on the Hammersmith and City Line (85), the four six-car units were introduced in 1936. This was the first surface stock to enter service with air-door equipment.

83

84

85

1935 Experimental and 1938 Standard Tube Stock

After the formation of the London Passenger Transport Board, the 1935/40 New Works programme was prepared which envisaged extensions to the Morden/Edgware Line (renamed the Northern Line in 1937) to Edgware and High Barnet, the electrification of the LNER Alexandra Palace branch and extensions to the Central Line. In anticipation of these extensions, four six-car trains of an experimental nature were ordered in 1935 from the Metropolitan-Cammell Carriage & Wagon Company. The new design incorporated many new features, the most obvious of which was the location of all electrical equipment beneath the underframe, thereby providing increased passenger carrying space. Three of the four car units were designed and built with semi-streamlined driving cabs (**86**), but the driving cab design was found to be unpopular with

the operating crews and reduced the passenger carrying capacity of the units. The fourth unit was designed with the conventional cab and flat end, very similar to that shown in (**87**) which illustrates one of the seven-car trains introduced as part of the 1938 standard stock delivery. At the same time, ten nine-car trains replaced earlier nine-car trains originally introduced on the Northern Line in November 1937.

The experimental 1935 stock, both streamlined and standard, entered operating service on the Piccadilly Line. It was withdrawn at the outbreak of World War II and stored. After the war, with the exception of the fourth train which was not streamlined, the semi-streamlined coaches were converted to trailer cars for operation with the 1938 stock. A train of standard 1938 stock is seen in Northern Line service emerging from the tunnels north of Hendon Central in (**89**). During 1949 driving motor car No 10306 was modified to provide better vision for standing passengers (**88**) but no further cars were so modified.

Metropolitan and District Modernisation

A new profile made its appearance on the District Line in 1937 when the first O stock was delivered for experimental service between High Street Kensington and Putney Bridge. Built by the Gloucester Carriage & Wagon Company Limited to replace earlier District and Metropolitan Railway Stock, the new coaches were of sleek appearance in marked contrast to their predecessors. Gone were the clerestory roofs and flat sided bodies of earlier stock, to be replaced by eliptical roofs, flush fitting windows and flared body panels. (**90**) illustrates one of the original two-car units. A second batch of cars designated P followed and eventually 570 cars were built of similar external design for use on the District and Circle Lines. The motor cars and trailers allocated to the District Line were fitted with different electrical equipment and designated Q. The external similarity of the Q and P stock can be seen by a comparison of (**91**) and (**92**), the former illustrating a District Line Q motor coach at South Kensington in 1958 and the latter illustrating a train of P stock on the Metropolitan Line at Harrow during the same decade.

The original interior of the O/P stock is illustrated in (**93**). The original O/P stock was originally fitted with metadyne control, but all units were converted to PCM equipment from 1955 onwards and thereafter designated CO/CP stock.

World War II

The outbreak of World War II on 3 September 1939 was to have a profound effect on the development of the London Underground system. Two days previously, London Transport Railways (together with all main-line railways) had come under Government Control under the provisions of the Emergency Powers (Defence) Act 1939 and in the following month (on 7 October) Pullman Car services were withdrawn — never to be restored — from the Metropolitan Line. In 1940, first class accommodation was withdrawn from Metropolitan and District Line trains (except for through trains to the Aylesbury and Watford joint lines) and London Transport's present one class system established.

Flooding occasioned by damage to the sections of the system under the River Thames was an obvious danger and, from 1 September, part of the Northern Line between Strand and Kennington was closed for three months to enable flood gates to be installed. At the same time, similar work was carried out on the City branch of the Northern Line, which was closed between London Bridge and Moorgate from 7 September 1939 to May 1940. The floodgates were under the control of a centre at Leicester Square and could be closed within 30 seconds of an air raid warning (**94**) being given, subject of course to no trains being within the section at the time. (**95**) illustrates one of the flood gates in operation, which were designed to resist a force of over 800 tons.

Inevitably, stock suffered from bombing and war damage and (**96**) shows a District Line Q trailer car No 013167 damaged in a 'blitz' in the autumn of 1940. Part of the car was subsequently salvaged and joined to a salvaged portion of a Metropolitan Line motor coach.

The tube stations themselves were of great value to Londoners in affording protection against bombing raids. Despite initial Government disapproval, thousands of Londoners flocked underground each night to escape the bombs, and as many as 177,000 were recorded on the night of 27 September

1940. Gradually, accommodation arrangements were improved under the organisation of J. P. Thomas, who had retired as General Manager (Railways) in 1938 but had been recalled for duty, and the installation of bunks and the distribution of reservations tickets improved the Londoners' lot (**97**). Safety could not, however, be assured even in the railway shelters, and during the war direct hits on stations at Trafalgar Square, Bounds Green, Balham and Bank each caused substantial numbers of deaths. Ironically, the worst underground disaster of the war occurred at an unopened station on the proposed extension to the Central Line and was not caused by direct bomb damage. In March 1943, 173 people were trampled to death when panic overcame crowds at Bethnal Green Station.

Elsewhere on the unopened Central Line eastern extension, in the incomplete tunnels between Leytonstone and Gants Hill, an aircraft component factory was operated by the Plessey Company (**98**). The factory was nearly five miles long and a small railway, the track of which can be seen on the left of the photograph, was operated for the transport of components.

96

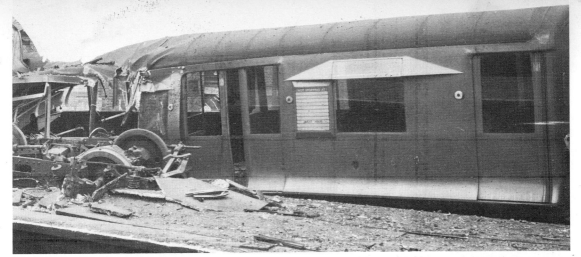

97

98

Tube Expansion

The greater part of the 1935/1940 New Works programme had been carried out before the commencement of war, including the extension of electrification on the Northern Line to East Finchley (**99**) in July 1939. Works continued on the electrification to High Barnet (April 1940), but ceased on the Finchley Central-Edgware branch once the line had been electrified as far as Mill Hill East in 1941. Work on the remainder of the Northern Line scheme under which it was proposed to extend underground trains to Bushey Heath was never resumed, although substantial works (**100**) including construction of viaducts and tunnels had already been commenced.

Work commenced again after the war, however, on the eastern extension of the Central Line and the first section between Liverpool Street and Stratford was brought into public use on 4 December 1946, having been opened on the previous day by the Minister of Transport, Mr Alfred Barnes, MP (**101**). In May 1947, tube trains were extended to Leytonstone (**102**) and thence partly over newly electrified ex-LNER lines and partly on new track, whilst in the west Central Line trains were extended from North Acton to Greenford in the following month and to West Ruislip in November 1948. In the east, the section

between Leytonstone and Newbury Park, the section used by the Plessey Company during the war, was opened in December 1947, when Gants Hill was provided with the impressive station illustrated in (**103**).

Electric services were extended as far as Epping in September 1949. Services were provided by 1923-30 standard stock, an example of which is seen in the mid-1950s in (**104**)

standing at Epping, adjacent to ex-GER Class F5 2-4-2T No 67193 on the Epping/Ongar steam shuttle which provided the connecting service until the line was electrified between these points in November 1957. The line between Epping and Ongar is single track, and its rural character can be clearly seen in (**105**) illustrating a Central Line train approaching the intermediate station, Blake Hall, in May 1971.

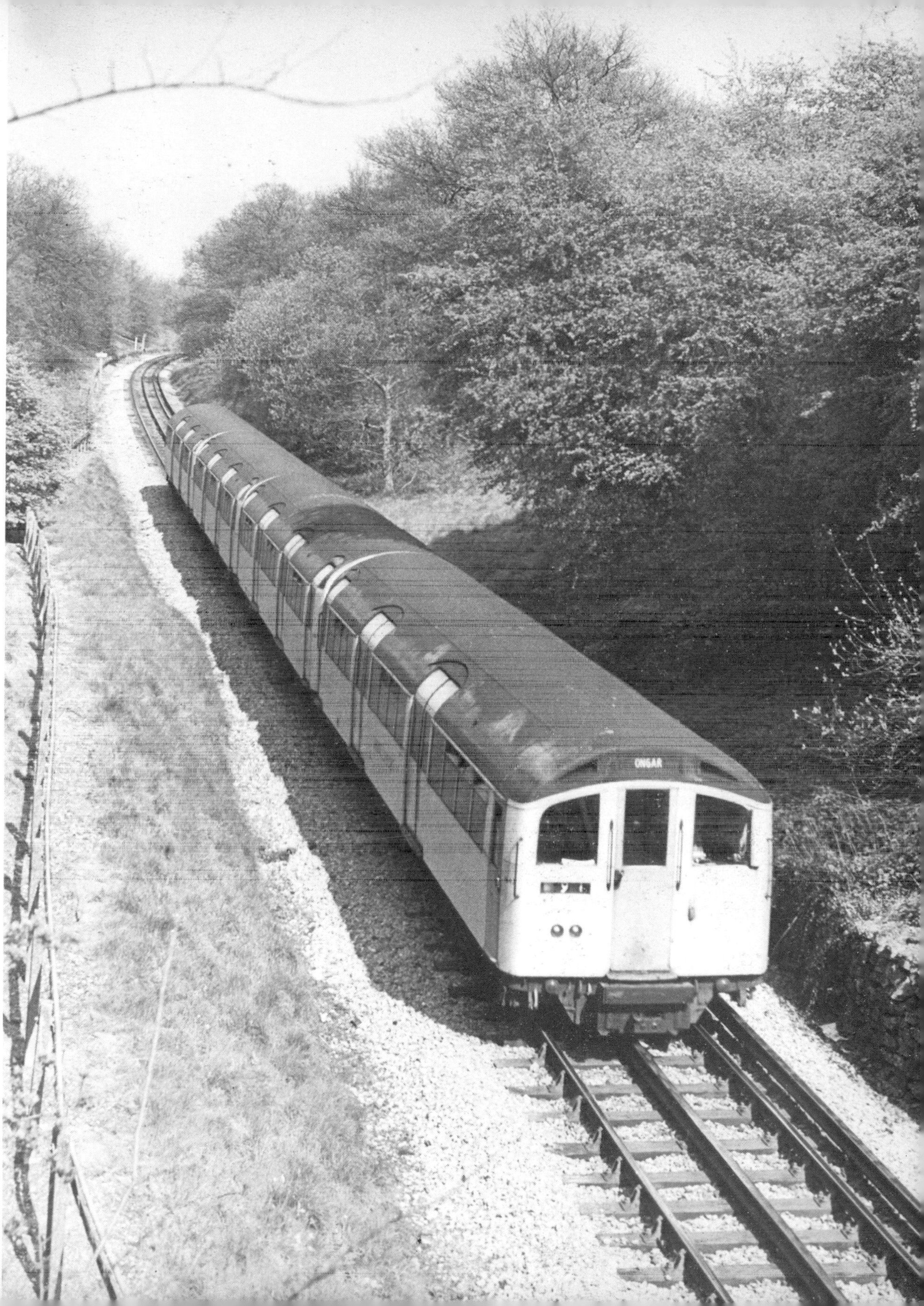
ONGAR

District Line R Stock

After the end of World War II, London Transport decided to withdraw all hand worked door stock, which meant that the renovated Circle stock (see **44**) and the District C, D, & E stock had to be replaced.

New trains of R stock were ordered composed entirely of motor cars but externally similar in appearance to the O/P stock. The newly built cars were designated R47, although they did not enter service until 1949, and subsequently additional stock designated R49 was ordered, the first of which entered service in May 1952. The R49 cars differed from the R47 cars in that the underframes and bodies were constructed of aluminium alloy and in the first R49 train one car (No 23567) was experimentally left unpainted when the other cars were painted in standard red livery. No adverse cleaning difficulties having

arisen, it was then decided to form a complete unpainted eight-car train, which went into operation in January 1953. Further cars designated R59 were delivered in unpainted light alloy in 1959, as shown in (**106**). The older cars operated with the new stock were painted aluminium to match — the painted leading motor car can be easily distinguished in the photograph — and it was subsequently decided that all R stock cars should be painted aluminium both to avoid the mixed aluminium/red formations illustrated in (**107**) at Farringdon in 1966 and to distinguish the same from CO/CP stock of similar external appearance. By 1968 all R stock had a similar aluminium appearance, although more recently a white livery has been adopted that is clearly shown in (**108**) which illustrates a District Line train entering Upminster Station from the sidings in August 1973.

1956/1959/1962 Tube Stock

Increased traffic on the Central and Piccadilly Lines led the LPTB seriously to consider the replacement of the pre-1938 tube stock. In 1956, three prototype trains were ordered from Metropolitan-Cammell Limited, Birmingham Railway Carriage & Wagon Limited and the Gloucester Railway Carriage & Wagon Company Limited. The specification included a number of innovations for tube trains, including unpainted aluminium alloy bodies, rubber suspension on the bogies and fluorescent lighting.The first prototype entered service on the Piccadilly Line in September 1957, and all three were in service by April 1958. (109) and (110) illustrate the exterior and interior respectively of the prototype unit. The cars have subsequently been renumbered and the illustrated cars numbered 42000 and 45001 are now numbered 1002 and 2002 respectively.

The 1956 prototypes proved successful and further trains of seven-car formation were ordered from Metropolitan-Cammell to replace the pre-1938 tube stock then operating on the Piccadilly Line and Central Line. The new stock was very similar to the prototypes, as can be seen from the exterior view illustrated in (111).

1960 Tube Stock

It had not originally been London Transport's intention to restock the Central Line with 1959 stock, as a new type of motor car had been in contemplation at the time. The probability of delays in development, however, led to this decision, although 12 prototype motor cars had been ordered in 1958 from Cravens Limited for operation on the Central Line. The new cars were of an entirely new design for tube working, and were fitted with four traction motors and a wheel spin protective device. More obvious to the travelling public was the provision of double width windows with a double glazing effect, details of which can be seen in the external and interior views illustrated in (112) and (113). The modern profile, now familiar to travellers on the Victoria Line, is particularly evident in the interior view. To work with the prototype motor coaches, 12 pre-1938 trailer cars were modernised at Acton Works to form three eight-car trains of a new formation for operation on the Central Line.

In 1963, five of the six 1960 tube stock four-car units were converted at Acton Works for use on the Woodford-Hainault branch of the Central Line during a full-scale trial of automatic train operation preparatory to its introduction on the Victoria Line. A four-coach train under automatic control is illustrated in (114). The modified ATO units can be recognised by the sealed up drivers door. Full scale trials commenced on Sunday 5 April 1964.

Amersham Stock

Modernisation plans during the 1950s were not confined to the tube sections of London Transport, as plans for the electrification of the Metropolitan beyond Rickmansworth to Amersham had been in existence since the 1935/1940 New Works programme. Certain parts of the programme had been completed before the outbreak of war, including the adoption of the Metropolitan Stanmore branch (opened in December 1932) as part of the Bakerloo service, but the proposed quadrupling and electrification works had not commenced. Metropolitan trains continued, therefore, to be electrically hauled as far as Rickmansworth, from which point the trains were steam hauled thence to Aylesbury or Chesham. (**115**) illustrates a Saturday through train between Liverpool Street and Chesham on the Chesham branch in 1954 hauled by ex-Great Central Railway 4-4-2T Class C13 No 67418, and (**116**) shows the standard Chesham branch train, formed of Ashbury stock, hauled by 2-6-2T No 41329 later in the decade.

As early as 1946, however, experimental coaches were built at Acton Works to obtain operating experience and passenger reaction preparatory to the electrification of the main-line to Amersham. Car No 17000 (**117**) was converted into a semi-open corridor saloon, the unique interior of which is illustrated in (**118**). After further interior alterations in 1949, it remained in passenger service until 1953.

117

18

Ultimately, an order was placed in 1959 with Cravens Limited for 248 cars, designated A60, to replace the T stock and locomotive hauled stock in use on the Metropolitan. This order was subsequently followed by a further order for 216 similar cars to replace the F stock on the Uxbridge lines (designated A62). The interior and exterior of the new stock is illustrated in (**119**) and (**120**). Not all the new stock had been delivered when electric trains began running to Chesham and Amersham on 12 September 1960 and (**121**) illustrates the first electric train made up of Metropolitan T stock to arrive at Chesham on a crew-training trip on 15 August. Through trains to Aylesbury, steam-hauled beyond Rickmansworth, continued to be provided

until Saturday 9 September 1961, one such being illustrated during the last week of steam operation in (**122**) hauled by an ex-LMSR 2-6-4T leaving Amersham. The modernisation of the Metropolitan Line involved not only electrification between Rickmansworth and Amersham/Chesham but also the provision of four tracks from Harrow-on-the-Hill to the Watford branch junction. Constructions works at Moor Park in 1961 are illustrated in (**123**) and the completed four-platform station can be seen in (**124**).

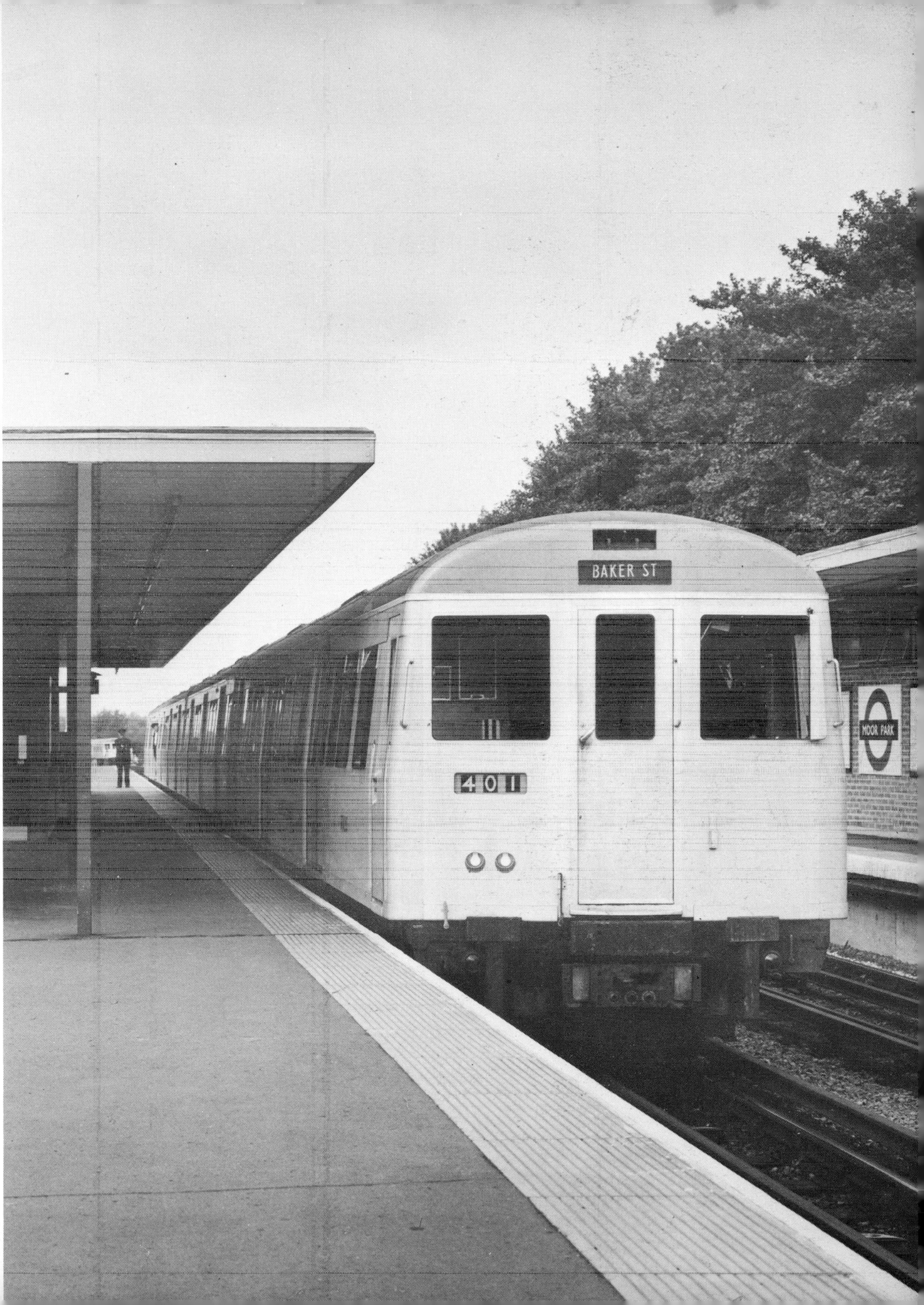
BAKER ST
401
MOOR PARK

The Centenary Celebrations

To mark the centenary of the opening of the Metropolitan Railway on 10 January 1863, London Transport arranged a 'grand parade' of rolling stock, past and present, at Neasden Depot on Thursday 23 May. Amongst invited guests who watched the grand parade from a specially constructed grandstand were the Chairman and Members of the London Transport Board, Members of Parliament and Civic Heads of areas served by the Metropolitan Line and chiefs of underground or urban rail systems in overseas cities, including New York, Moscow and Tokyo. Before the assembled multitude were paraded 15 trains representing various types of steam and electric locomotives and rolling stock which had operated on underground services during the preceding century. The parade was led by the 97-year old Metropolitan 4-4-0T locomotive No 23 (**125**), to which were attached two open wagons in which members of the London Transport Musical & Dramatic Society re-enacted the special trip attended by Mr Gladstone and others illustrated in (**4**). No 23 was pushed by a battery

locomotive. The second train in the parade (**126**) was made up of Metropolitan E class 0-4-4T No L44 (originally Metropolitan Railway No 1) hauling a late nineteenth century milk van and four Ashbury coaches then recently withdrawn from service on the Chesham branch and then, as now, in the ownership of the Bluebell Railway in Sussex. The third historical train in the procession (**127**) was made up of Metropolitan Bo-Bo electric locomotive No 1 *John Lyon* hauling six coaches of 'Steam' stock in service until 1961 on the through trains to Aylesbury. Further examples of London Transport stock were also exhibited, including Metropolitan T stock, the last of which was withdrawn in October 1962, District F stock, London Transport P and A60 stock, together with tube trains of pre-1938, 1938 and 1959 vintage. Metropolitan 0-6-2T F class locomotive No L52 (previously Metropolitan No 93) and ex-GWR 0-6-0PT No L98 (formerly No 7739) were also in the parade hauling engineers trains.

A plaque to commemorate the 1863 opening of the line was unveiled at Baker Street on the following day.

26

27

The Victoria Line

Statutory powers for the construction of the Victoria Line were contained in the British Transport Commission Act 1955, but authorisation for commencement of works was not granted until 1962. As the last new tube railway across Central London had been opened more than 50 years previously, contracts were placed by London Transport in anticipation of the 1962 authorisation for the construction of two experimental tunnels in 1960. Designed to form part of the Victoria Line when built, the tunnels were constructed between Finsbury Park and Manor House and between Netherton Road (Tottenham) and Manor House, and the experiments enabled comparisons to be made between flexible-jointed cast-iron lining and concrete lining designed by London Transport's two firms of consulting engineers. Examples of the two types of construction are shown in (**128**) and (**129**).

Whereas the majority of Londoners were unaware of the experimental tunnelling work being carried out on the northern part of the line, few Londoners could remain unaware of the new works after the first weekend in August 1963, during which London Transport engineers and contractors built an 'umbrella' bridge weighing 600 tons and covering an area of 2,500sq yd over Oxford Circus (**130**) to enable a new upper concourse for the new Oxford Circus underground station to be built underneath. The umbrella remained a feature of the London scene for nearly five years.

Orders for new rolling stock were placed with the Metropolitan-Cammell Carriage & Wagon Company Limited in 1964, and 244 motor and trailer cars were ordered. The new cars closely resembled, both externally and internally, the 1960

128

129

130

experimental motor cars introduced on the Central Line and subsequently converted for automatic train control, although the Victoria Line motor coaches were easily distinguishable by the wrap-round windows provided in the drivers cabs (**131**). The stock commenced passenger service between Walthamstow Central and Highbury and Islington on 1 September 1968. The next section thence to Warren Street opened three months later, and the main section between Warren Street and Victoria was opened by HM Queen Elizabeth II on 7 March 1969. After her opening speech, in which the Queen recalled that the first electric tube railway had been opened by her great grandfather in 1890, the Queen travelled between Green Park and Oxford Circus in the cab of a special train and returned thence to Victoria as a passenger.

The Queen's great-great grandmother was commemorated by murals at Victoria Station, as an imaginative feature of the new line was the provision of special motifs incorporated in the tiling at each station to identify it easily to regular passengers (**132**).

New Circle Line Stock

After completion of the delivery of the A60 and A62 stock to the Metropolitan Line, London Transport placed an order in 1968 with Metropolitan-Cammell Limited for 35 six-car trains (and two spare cars) for use on the Circle and Hammersmith and City service. Designated C69 stock in the optimistic anticipation of its delivery in 1969, the new stock externally resembled the coaches constructed for the Amersham electrification. The two types are, however, easily distinguishable; the C69 stock is provided with four pairs of double doors to expedite passenger movements on the intensive Circle Line service, and the newer stock is fitted with a ventilation system similar to that installed on the Victoria Line coaches obviating the need for hinged ventilators on the exterior. The interior and exterior of the C69 stock is illustrated in (**133**) and (**134**) respectively, the latter showing a Hammersmith to Whitechapel train approaching Royal Oak Station in April 1973.

The introduction of the C69 stock enabled the Q stock on the District Line to be replaced by CO/CP stock from the Hammersmith and City Line, and Circle Line and Hammersmith and City Line trains are now served solely by the new vehicles. (135) illustrates CP stock on Hammersmith and City Line duties before the introduction of C69 stock in 1965, passing over the original tracks between Moorgate and Aldersgate which were replaced by new tracks under a concrete covered way shown on the right to facilitate the development of the Barbican Area in

December of that year. Most of Moorgate Circle and Widened Lines station is now submerged under modern office development, but its earlier appearance is illustrated in (136), which shows the station in 1952. On the left, two Metropolitan trains formed of T stock prepare to head for Watford; on the right ex-LNER Class N2 0-6-2T No 69581 and ex-LMSR 2-6-2T No 40028 (both fitted with condensing gear) prepare to leave for Welwyn Garden City and St Albans respectively.

Steam's Last Fling

As we have seen earlier, the greater part of London Transport's fleet of shunting locomotives was inherited from the Metropolitan Railway. The class E and F tank engines had been delivered at about the turn of the century and they were becoming increasingly expensive and difficult to maintain by the mid-1950s. In 1956/7, therefore, London Transport acquired from the Western Region of British Railways two 0-6-0 pannier tanks to replace two F class 0-6-2T. Ex-GWR Nos 7711 and 5752 were re-numbered as London Transport L90 and L91, in which guise the latter is shown in (**137**) at Neasden in July 1957. Between 1957 and 1963, 11 further pannier tanks were purchased from British Railways and numbered L89-L99

(Nos L90/91 being used on two separate occasions). The locomotives were used for shunting purposes and regularly on the 'tip' or 'dump' train between Neasden Depot and Croxley on which L94 (ex-GWR No 7752) is seen approaching Moor Park in (**138**) in August 1968.

Perhaps fittingly, as the original trains on the Metropolitan Railway had been hauled by Great Western locomotives in 1863, the last steam train on London's underground was hauled also by an ex-GWR locomotive. In (**139**) L94 is seen posing for photographers and enthusiasts at Barbican Station with 'The Last Steam Train on the Underground' on Sunday, 6 June 1971, three years after the end of standard gauge steam on British Railways.

THE LAST STEAM TRAIN ON THE UNDERGROUND 544

42

Further Modern Tube Stock

Continuing its policy of replacing prewar rolling stock, in 1972 London Transport introduced 30 new 7-car tube trains on the Northern Line similar to those constructed for the Victoria Line, although not fitted for automatic operation. A further 33 trains of Mark 2 1972 Tube Stock were also delivered to the Northern Line although destined for eventual use on the Jubilee Line. These trains (**140**) have various livery changes compared to the earlier 1972 Tube Stock.

The cab ends of the second batch of Northern Line trains retained the 'all silver appearance' of the earlier stock and Victoria Line stock, unlike the new six-car trains intended for the Piccadilly Line known as '1973 tube stock', the first of which was delivered to the West Ruislip Depot in 1974 (**141**). The new Piccadilly Line trains are longer than previous stock and, with the extension to Heathrow Airport in mind, were designed with enhanced performance and provision for baggage in the 'stand back' areas alongside the doors. The most important technical innovation in the new Piccadilly Line stock is the first use by London Transport of the Westcode electrically-controlled brake in place of conventional electro-pneumatic equipment.

Both the Mark 2 1972 Tube Stock and the 1973 Tube Stock are designed for eventual one man operation.

The interior of a trailer car of the 1973 tube stock, showing the widened entrance vestibules intended to cope with passengers' luggage, is illustrated in (**142**). Piccadilly Line trains were extended from Hounslow West to Hatton Cross, the intermediate station towards Heathrow Airport, on 19 July, 1975 and the final extension to Heathrow Central (**143**) was opened in 1977.

43

London Transport Architecture

Most passengers on London's Underground probably give little thought to the architecture of the railway stations through which they pass, particularly since most of the tube station platforms are basically similar in appearance. The system is endowed, however, with a vast variety of stations, although probably the most unusual structure to be erected as a consequence of the development of the Underground system is the house number 23/24 Leinster Gardens in Bayswater (**144**). Built by the Metropolitan Railway during the construction of the extension from Edgware Road to Westminster (opened 1868) to preserve the continuity of the Square, numbers 23/24 Leinster Gardens are dummy houses formed only of a front wall and, surprisingly perhaps after two World Wars, still survive today.

The original stations constructed by the Metropolitan &

District Railways in the days of steam were designed in spacious style, in keeping with main-line railway practice of the time and to facilitate the dispersal of steam from the tunnels. This spaciousness is well illustrated in (**145**) which shows Barbican Station (formerly Aldersgate Street and Barbican) on the section of the line opened in 1865. This station is all the more capacious because of the presence of the Widened Lines whilst the photograph interestingly illustrates the diamond shaped name-boards that preceded the roundels with which travellers are familiar today.

Possibly the greatest contrast ever to have existed on the London Transport system with the grandeur of the original Metropolitan and District Line stations is to be found in Wood Siding (**146**), one of the intermediate stations on the Brill branch, photographed, so far as one can infer from the advertisements on the station 'building', at the time of World

14

149

War I. The station proudly displays its Metropolitan ownership and links with the Great Central Railway as, in common with all Metropolitan Lines north of Harrow, it had come under the management of the Metropolitan and Great Central Joint Committee on 2 April 1906.

The station at Wood Siding has long since disappeared, but modern travellers will recognise the architecture of the Hampstead Tube illustrated in (**147**). Although South Kentish Town Station closed in June 1924, the style of architecture can still be seen elsewhere on the Northern Line, for instance at Goodge Street.

Another closed station is illustrated in (**148**). St John's Wood Road (latterly called Lords) was the first station beyond Baker Street on the Metropolitan Line extension to Swiss Cottage opened in April 1868. As traffic on the Metropolitan Line expanded and the line from Finchley Road to Wembley Park was quadrupled, the tunnels between Baker Street and Finchley

Road became a bottleneck and as early as 1925 plans were afoot for the construction of a new line from a point near Kilburn and Brondesbury Station to Edgware Road on the Inner Circle, with a view to which Edgware Road (Met) was rebuilt in 1926. The new tunnel was never built but the problem was solved (after the formation of the LPTB) by the construction of an extension of the Bakerloo Line between Baker Street and Finchley Road (opened on 20 November 1939) and the transfer of Stanmore branch workings to that new line.

New stations were constructed on the new Bakerloo Link, as a result of which St John's Wood was renamed Lords in June 1939; the modern exterior of St John's Wood (Bakerloo Line) is illustrated in (**149**). It had been intended that Lords Station would be retained for access to the MCC cricket ground but, because of the outbreak of World War II, both Lords and the other intermediate station — Marlborough Road — were closed on the opening of the new Bakerloo Line.

15

Piccadilly Line Extension Constrasts

The Eastern and Western extensions of the Piccadilly Line in 1932 and 1933 necessitated the construction of a number of new stations and the rebuilding of others, particularly on the section between Hammersmith and Northfields where the existing District Railway tracks were quadrupled to provide express Piccadilly Line services. (**150**) illustrates South Harrow Station, on the ex-District Line to which Piccadilly Line services

were extended on 4 July 1932, not long after the introduction of the LT double decker bus standing at the station on route 158 to Watford. The photograph was taken about three were extended on 4 July 1932, not long after the photograph of the impressive station at Arnos Grove illustrated in (**151**) opened in March 1933 on the Northern extension of the Piccadilly Line. Illustrated in (**152**) is the heavy architecture of the western Piccadilly Line terminus at Uxbridge, to which the line was extended in October 1933 to augment the District Line service that had commenced 30 years previously.

153

154

Works and Depots

London's numerous underground trains require, of course, constant attention and overhaul, and major repairs are carried out at six main depots: Neasden (Metropolitan and Bakerloo Lines); Ealing Common (District); Golders Green (Northern); Northfields (Piccadilly); West Ruislip (Central); and Northumberland Park (Victoria).

Save for Golders Green and Ealing Common, the latter of which is illustrated in (153), all the main depots are of modern construction. The aerial photograph of Ealing Common well illustrates the large acreage that is required for a main depot, whilst more modern facilities are illustrated by the exterior of Upminster Depot (154) and the interior of Northumberland Park (155).

Great is the contrast between the modern depots and the early District Line facilities illustrated at South Harrow in (156), whilst no longer are steam locomotives serviced at Lillie Bridge or at Neasden at which 0-6-0PT Nos L98, L91 and L97 are seen in (157) after withdrawal from service.

Posters

A selection of London Transport Posters. (**158**) 'Too Much of a Good Thing' — 1910. (**159**) 'Hello! Did you Come by Underground?' by Mabel Lucy Attwell — 1913. (**160**) 'Move to Edgware' — 1924. (**161**) 'Turning the Wheels of War'. (**162**) Central Line Extensions — December 1948. (**163**) 'We Londoners' — 1961. (**164**) 'Opening of the Brixton Extension of the Victoria Line' — 1968 and (**165**) 'Fly the Tube' — 1977.

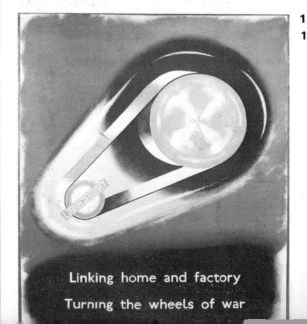

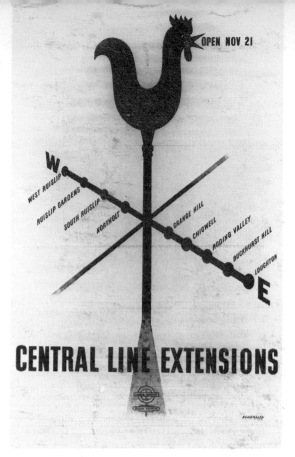

OPEN NOV 21

W
WEST RUISLIP
RUISLIP GARDENS
SOUTH RUISLIP
NORTHOLT
GRANGE HILL
CHIGWELL
RODING VALLEY
BUCKHURST HILL
LOUGHTON
E

CENTRAL LINE EXTENSIONS

WE LONDONERS . . .

London Transport is proud to present a display of its more decorative passengers for the interest of the more soberly dressed. No prizes are offered for naming these types correctly, but they are all authentic and can all be 'collected' by bus or Underground.

VICTORIA LINE

VICTORIA
DISTRICT LINE
PIMLICO
VAUXHALL
STOCKWELL
Clapham Common
Clapham North
NORTHERN LINE
BRIXTON

The picture completed
BRIXTON EXTENSION NOW OPEN

Fly the Tube

HEATHROW CENTRAL

Take the Piccadilly Line to Heathrow Airport.
It's the only way to fly.

Photo Credits

Below: The Metropolitan Railway opposed its incorporation in the LPTB in 1933 on the grounds that it was a main-line railway providing express and goods services and not merely urban short haul passenger services. Metropolitan Railway Class K 2-6-4T was introduced primarily for freight working, on which duty No 115 leads a goods train away from the LMS exchange sidings at Verney Junction in 1936.

AMERSHAM
CHESHAM

WATFORD

WATFORD JUNCTION

MILL

MOOR PARK
NORTHWOOD
NORTHWOOD HILLS
PINNER
NORTH HARROW
HARROW-ON-THE-HILL

HATCH END
HEADSTONE LANE
HARROW & WEALDSTONE
KENTON
PRESTON ROAD

STANMORE
CANONS PARK
QUEENSBURY
KINGSBURY

EDGWARE
BURNT OAK
COLINDALE
HENDON CENTRAL
BRENT CROSS

WEST RUISLIP

HILLINGDON

RUISLIP MANOR
RAYNERS LANE

WEST HARROW
NORTHWICK PARK

WEMBLEY PARK
NEASDEN
DOLLIS HILL
WILLESDEN GREEN
KILBURN

GOLDERS GREEN
HAMPST

UXBRIDGE ICKENHAM RUISLIP EASTCOTE

RUISLIP GARDENS

SOUTH RUISLIP

NORTHOLT

GREENFORD

PERIVALE

HANGER LANE

SOUTH HARROW
SUDBURY HILL
SUDBURY TOWN
ALPERTON

SOUTH KENTON
NORTH WEMBLEY
WEMBLEY CENTRAL
STONEBRIDGE PARK
HARLESDEN
WILLESDEN JUNCTION
KENSAL GREEN

BELS

WEST HAMPSTEAD
FINCHLEY ROA
SWISS CO
ST. JOH

QUEEN'S PARK
KILBURN PARK

MAIDA VALE
WARWICK AVENUE

EDGWARE ROAD
MARYLEBONE

PARK ROYAL

NORTH EALING

EALING BROADWAY

LADBROKE GROVE

WESTBOURNE PARK

ROYAL OAK

PADDINGTON
BAYSWATER
NOTTING HILL GATE

EDGWARE ROAD

BAKER STREET

GR
PORTL
STR
REGE

EALING COMMON

SOUTH EALING
NORTHFIELDS

BOSTON MANOR
OSTERLEY

HOUNSLOW EAST
HOUNSLOW CENTRAL
HOUNSLOW WEST

HATTON CROSS

HEATHROW CENTRAL

EAST ACTON

WEST ACTON
NORTH ACTON
WHITE CITY

GOLDHAWK ROAD

ACTON TOWN

LATIMER ROAD
HOLLAND PARK

SHEPHERD'S BUSH
SHEPHERD'S BUSH

KENSINGTON ▲ (OLYMPIA)

HIGH STREET KENSINGTON
KNIGHTSBRIDGE

QUEENSWAY
LANCASTER GATE

MARBLE ARCH

BOND STREET

GREEN PARK

HYDE PARK CORNER

MARBLE ARCH

P

CHISWICK PARK

HAMMERSMITH

BARONS COURT

GLOUCESTER ROAD

SLOANE SQUARE

ST. JAMES'S

KEW GARDENS

RICHMOND

GUNNERSBURY

TURNHAM GREEN
STAMFORD BROOK
RAVENSCOURT PARK

WEST KENSINGTON

EARL'S COURT

SOUTH KENSINGTON

VICTORIA

WEST BROMPTON

PIMLICO

FULHAM BROADWAY

PARSONS GREEN

PUTNEY BRIDGE

RIVER THAMES

ST
CLAPHAM
CLAPHAM COMMC
CLAPHAM SOUTH
BALHAM
TOOTING BEC
TOOTING BROADWAY
COLLIER'S WOOD
SOUTH WIMBLEDON
MORDEN

EAST PUTNEY

SOUTHFIELDS

WIMBLEDON PARK

WIMBLEDON